ISBN: 978-0-578-12828-3

Dedication

This book is dedicated to my daughters, granddaughters, nieces and great nieces. It is my prayer that they and their friends will enjoy reading and learning the do's and don'ts of proper attire. While this book focuses mainly on proper workplace attire, many scenarios also are relevant to attire outside of the workplace.

Contents

Acknowledgements

Thanks to my husband of 26 years, Tayro Christanio, for supporting me as I aspire to be all that I can be.

Thanks to my beautiful Niece Erika D. Warnick for editing a version of this book. Erika commented, **"This book is a timely topic."**

Thanks to my fabulous sister Ann "Bobbie" Chambers, who also edited a version of this book. Bobbie's comment: **"I like it!"**

Thanks to my lifelong friend and former boss professor Deborah Scott. Deborah, who provided an edit of this book, said **"I like it and *many* young women could use this tool!"** Thanks, Deb, I will be forever grateful.

Pamela de la Fuente supported me with writing the foreword and providing the final edit **"Fantastic information for working women,"** Pamela said.

Last, but certainly not least, thanks to my family members and co-workers who inspired me to write this book. Sometimes we need a little boost to get our creative juices flowing. Thanks!

My daily motto: Live, love and laugh!

Foreword

Sometimes women – young and old – just don't realize what we're doing wrong when it comes to work wardrobes.

Many young women graduate college not knowing how to dress for the office. *Do I dress like I'm going to church? Do I dress like I'm going to class?* Joyce answers the questions of what to wear and how to wear it in "Dressing Classy Doesn't Change."

Likewise, many women who have been in the working world for years might not realize they're committing fashion don'ts. I've been guilty a time or two of chipped toenail polish, wrinkles and ashy feet. This book gave me a wake-up call. These things are not acceptable.

Corporate America needs more female executives. Having experience and ability are key to getting ahead, but having a professional look will help more than you think.

You could be asked to a meeting with an executive at any time, Joyce tells us. You have to be ready – and so does your outfit.

Pamela E. Spencer de la Fuente

Professional writer and editor

Introduction

First I want to let you know that my corporate career has spanned more than 23 years. I currently work for a major corporation in a management role within the diversity department.

My position requires frequent travel to corporate conferences, events and meetings with clients and vendors.

I have attended conferences with female facilitators presenting workshops on topics including healthy eating and business networking skills. Too often, I have seen attire that begged for improvement.

As I observed speakers and attendees in clothes that would be more appropriate for a different setting, I visualized becoming a public speaker traveling abroad, boosting women's self-esteem by providing advice on appropriate workplace attire. This desire, mingled with inspiration from my peers, friends and family, prompted me to write this book.

Several times I have been approached by peers suggesting that I start a business to teach women how to dress appropriately in the workplace. While I'm an avid shopper with a keen eye for fashion, I've never professed to be one of the world's greatest fashion gurus. However, others saw something in me that I didn't see in myself.

On several occasions, I've been asked to provide guidance to women in the workplace as to what constitutes professional attire.

Once at a corporate meeting, I was shocked to see the attire of the female executive who facilitated the meeting. She wore white hip-hugger jeans that were very tight and wrinkled with a flowered blouse half tucked into her low-rise waistline – no jacket. Quickly after the meeting, a co-worker stopped by my office recommending, for the third time, that I start a business to teach women how to dress.

I recall often seeing women in outfits that made me shake my head and say, "Um, um, um." Not because I was judging them. I simply believe that if they had the knowledge and information about professional attire, they gladly would take advantage of it.

One of the smartest women I know, Ms. Collier, who analyzes *everything, everywhere*, repeatedly has recommended that I pursue a career as a celebrity stylist.

Then there are my five beautiful sisters, Ann "Bobbie," Creamola "Crea," Emma, Linda and Veronica "Beb." They have always complimented my attire. Linda has recommended that I start a consignment shop (with clothes from my closet), Beb thinks I should become a stylist for the Atlanta housewives. Emma thinks I'm a fashion queen. My smile is broad and I am filled with gratitude as I reflect on the love, encouragement and support from my sisters. Also, I want to thank my sisters Bobbie and Creamola for loaning me their fashionable clothes during my younger years.

Bobbie, who lives in Pennsylvania, once overnighted me her full-length fur coat to wear to a New Year's Eve party in Missouri – thank you, sister! Although Creamola wore a larger size than me, I was *always* trying to find something that I could borrow from her closet. I would go to many lengths to keep up with the latest fashion.

I would be remiss not to mention a once-close girlfriend, Olivia, whom I haven't seen in many years. She taught me how to select quality fabrics. I learned to identify linen, silk and other luxurious materials that hung far on the other side of department stores. Thank you, Olivia.

Also, Jan, better known as "Ms. St. John," do I need to say more?

Last, but definitely not least, my two queen bees, my daughters! Monica Mabery-Henderson and A'Keela Mabery-Williams. They have always looked to me to show them what dressing classy entails. They've grown into beautiful butterflies creating their own hot and classy styles. Go, Monie and Keela! But it doesn't stop there. My granddaughters, Bobbi, Brooke, and Brilyn also are observing others and learning classy fashion techniques.

I believe readers will be able to visualize the different scenarios referenced throughout this book. Some are serious and some will make you laugh. I tell it like it is. Overall, I believe the information is useful and will benefit seasoned professionals and young ladies for generations to come. Many styles may change, but DRESSING CLASSY DOESN'T CHANGE.

This book is focused on fictitious scenarios and is not written to describe any specific women.

I was shocked to see the attire of the female executive who facilitated the meeting .

Chapter 1: Defining Classy

Classy is defined by Webster's dictionary as "Having elegance or taste or refinement in manners or dress." Because I like these two words, I would also add "stylish and "admirably smart."

"Business Casual" Not Clearly Defined

Employees in today's work environment are able to dress more casually than employees in previous years. However, most corporations do not clearly define the term "business casual." Different people interpret "appropriate" workplace attire in different ways. This can frustrate employers trying to maintain a consistently professional work environment.

There is a very thin line between employers harassing, versus correcting, their employees regarding attire. As such, the subject of what is appropriate work attire is rarely addressed. However, dressing casual doesn't mean one should substitute dressing classy.

Executive Presence

An October 29, 2012, Forbes article called "Do You Have Executive Presence?" caught my eye. The article discusses a study done by the Center for Talent Innovation, a nonprofit research organization in New York.

More than three-quarters of senior executives surveyed said "unkempt attire" distracts from executive presence, according to the article. Executive presence is the ability to project gravitas – confidence and poise under pressure and decisiveness, the article said.

> **More than three-quarters of senior executives said "unkempt attire" distracts from executive presence.**

Chapter 2: What People are Saying About Corporate Dress Policies

In researching corporate dress policies on the Internet, I found the following interesting excerpts about workplace attire. The first bullet point is an actual corporate policy while others are excerpts from conversations between supervisors and/or employees.

Some of them are humorous and I couldn't help but chuckle. Fictitious names used to hide identities were purposely omitted.

- *Employees project our corporation's professionalism and the quality of our products and services, so it's important that our appearance and attire reflect that. Dress codes may vary based on your role and location. For example, employees interfacing with customers have a specific dress code. Your manager can assist with questions regarding your applicable dress policy.*

- *I don't think you'll find any such thing in writing (dress policy). Any attempt to dictate appropriate work attire will probably end up in a lawsuit (especially if the supervisor type is a male specifying what is appropriate for a female and vice versa). Most workplaces have no official guidance on appropriate dress, only suggestions such as "business attire," or "business casual."*

- *Now I am being told that the dress code for employees is at the discretion of the local managers; as wrong as I know that sounds I would like for someone to point me to specific regulations or anything within the Code of Regulations, so if this becomes an issue I will at least be armed with the black and white explanations.*

- *I don't see dress codes so much of a problem with the male gender as I do with the female gender. I'm disappointed in how many of the women dress. If they only looked more closely in the mirror to see how badly they look. We have a young gal in our office and sometimes, it's really shocking. I blame management for letting her wear such clothing. Sometimes she comes in with tights and an open sweater that ends at her waist. This day, the sweater was open and exposed much of her lower body.*
  So maybe I'm old fashioned. Maybe some customers really like this type of dress. And maybe, some are terribly offended.

- *When a woman wears such short dresses, tight dresses, low cut dresses – with a body that really doesn't fit in the clothing, it's an eyesore. Forget the offensiveness ...*

just a boring eyesore. ***** hanging out has a place … but not in a professional office.

I'm ready for all the criticism … I'm from the Baby Boomer generation so it's hard to convince me that this type of attire is OK. As long as managers permit it, eyesores will continue. I'm just really grateful that I had a good mother who taught me how to dress and I passed that on to my daughter.

- *You got to choose your battles! Remember your local managers are the ones that write and sign off on your appraisals. Do you really want your appraisal, and possible awards, to suffer just so that you can wear more comfortable clothes?*

- *That's why, as a supervisor, I keep my eyes to myself and my mouth shut. As long as the person can do his or her work and knows when to dress appropriately for visitors, I leave it alone.*

- *We had a woman who wore shorts (nice, cotton type) to work almost every day. She had frequent customer contact, but the office was non-air-conditioned and very oppressive during the summer months. Her supervisor suggested one day that she dress more "professional" because of the nature of her job. Her answer was "When you pay me enough to afford such clothes, I'll consider wearing them." End of conversation. The subject was never brought up again.*

As you can see from the above excerpts, the subject matter of appropriate workplace attire is a major issue, but it is often overlooked. But the excerpts are not what led me to write this book. Read on to see what inspired me to start writing.

> *Any attempt to dictate appropriate work attire will probably end up in a lawsuit (especially if the supervisor type is a male specifying what is appropriate for a female and vice versa).*

Chapter 3: Loving Fashion

Feel Deserving

I can't deny that I love, love, love fashion. When I told my girlfriend that I purchased a pair of Christian Louboutin boots (the designer of the expensive, classy brand that stars such as Oprah Winfrey wear), she looked at me as if to say, "You have lost your mind." I had to laugh at myself.

The boots were a luxury purchase and I felt deserving after years of working, raising two beautiful daughters, making sacrifices and helping out with my grandchildren.

By no means am I suggesting you must spend big bucks on clothing and shoes in order to dress classy. I know there are many affordable options and I continue to choose those options. Your budget should always be a consideration. I've been a fashion connoisseur for a long time and I've learned how to dress classy and appropriately. I am pleased to share a few tips with you.

Styles Change …

… but dressing classy doesn't change. For example:

- **Shoe heels** are getting taller, soles are thicker and patterns are wilder. Toes out, heels out, some may lace or buckle up your leg -- some are suitable for work -- some aren't.

- **Boots** range from covering women's ankles to covering their thighs. Some are sexy, some dressy, some comfy, some casual — some may ruin your image.

- **Dresses** get shorter, colors get bolder and fabrics become more revealing. Some are spandex, free flowing, low cut, some have thin or no straps, some short, some long — choose wisely for the occasion and season.

- **Pants** come with slim and wide legs. Pants come in all colors of the rainbow. Some fabrics are tight, some are stretchy — some may require we cover our hips.

- **Jackets** come short in length, they come long, some have one button, some have many, some have a slender cut, vents in the back, long sleeves or short sleeves — the right size is key.

- **Fabrics** range from $1 a yard to designer prices far beyond our imagination. However, fabric is the key to classy attire. The saying "You get what you pay for" definitely applies to fabric.

- **Colors** should be carefully blended. Normally, blending three colors or fewer in the workplace is safe. Additionally, certain colors can make you appear larger than you are -- beware!

- **Hosiery** is sold in many patterns and colors. Some hosiery is appropriate for the office, some styles are more appropriate for after-hours events.

- **Belts** are sold in many styles. There are stretch belts, cloth belts, leather belts, pleather (fake leather) belts, wide belts, narrow belts and belts with bling — be cautious of your selection.

Chapter 4: Let's Begin With Dressing the Feet
High Heels

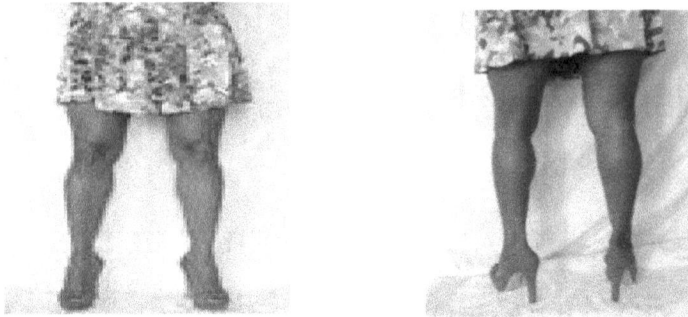

Wearing 4- to 6-inch heels with a mini-dress is a definite office no-no. This style shoe is appropriate when worn with a dress that is no more than 2 inches above the knee or with a pantsuit. Mini-dresses are always a no-no.

If you are wearing a rainbow-colored outfit, it is not necessary to try and match it with a rainbow-colored shoe. I've seen this scenario work in very few instances. Stick to a solid color. Also, flip-flops are not sandals and are not professional attire. Flip-flops are for casual weekend wear only.

Animal-print or multicolor shoes should be worn with corporate solid colors such as black, brown, cream, navy, beige or gray. This tidbit of advice may seem to many as conservative and boring, but classy is key. Also ladies, polish your shoes – scuffed shoes, even if it's only the heel or toe tip of your shoe – are tacky. Remember, shoes complement your outfit and serve as an accessory.

Shoes that lace or buckle up the leg should never be worn in the workplace. These styles are more appropriate for after-hours events or the weekend.

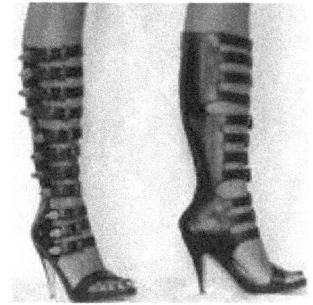

I was once told that if your feet hurt, you are looking good. However, if the shoes are too small, leave them in the store or give them away to charity. I've heard men comment negatively about women tiptoeing because their feet hurt. I've also heard men talk about how horrible it looks for a woman's toes or heels to hang over shoes. You cannot be looking your best while suffering from all of this pain. Is the pain really worth ruining your feet?

While we are on the subject of feet, get a pedicure (do it yourself or go to a professional) before wearing your toes out. For the record, polish peeling off your toenails is *not* classy. No matter how hurried you are, definitely use a cream or lotion on your entire foot after every shower. Do you really want your feet to look as though you've been running in sand on a beach? I am not implying that you are trying to impress men in the office or elsewhere, this is just information I believe will be helpful to you. Many men are attracted to women's feet and shoes.

Boots

Thigh-high boots (or any boot extending above the knee) with a 4- to 6-inch heel do not project a professional image in the workplace. This style is sexy and you may receive many compliments, but again, this style boot should be worn after hours or on weekends. Remember the movie "Pretty Woman" with Julia Roberts? The actress portrayed a woman on the stroll, need I say more? I am not saying do not wear boots, they can add flare to an outfit and can be appropriate in a professional environment. Just consider the image you seek to project.

A lower-heel boot that covers the knee, like the one pictured on the right, can be appropriate for casual workdays or with the right dress.

You know those popular boots for cold weather? The ones with the fur and thick rubber soles? Those are appropriate for cold weather outside, but not all day in the office. I believe this type of boot was designed specifically for warmth, not fashion. As such, bring a pair of shoes to change into after you are in the building.

Ankle boots are tricky. Some are dressy and look great with shorter-length outfits. Others can ruin a nice outfit.

Ensure that the fabric of your outfit and the boot complement one another. For instance, if you are wearing a silk, dressy polyester or classy knit (such as a St. John Knit) outfit, ensure that the boot has a slim, feminine toe or heel. If you are wearing a thick fabric such as wool or heavy knit, it is OK to wear a less feminine dressy-style boot that may have a thick sole and a round toe. Pants or long skirts work well with ankle boots.

Cowgirl boots are to be worn with casual dresses or skirts in fabrics such as jean, khaki, wool or leather – do not wear these boots with polyester or silk outfits. Blouses in any fabric, along with a pair of blue jeans, can be worn with these boots. Also, be careful wearing cowgirl boots with mini-dresses – women with toned legs can look classy in this style. Legs that are very thin or very thick normally can't pull off this style.

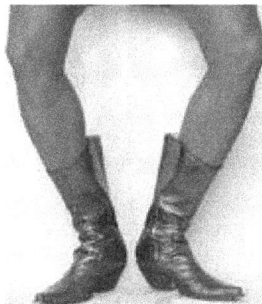

Chapter 5: Dressing the Body

Dresses

Dresses are the standard for femininity, yet some have taken the class out of this attire. While the current trend is to skip the hosiery, if you wear a dress too short without pantyhose, you remove the grace from the attire. Wearing a knee-length or longer dress does not require pantyhose. However, a dress 2 inches or more above the knee requires pantyhose; sheer dresses may also require you wear a slip. The same rule applies to skirts. I know your legs may be shapely and sexy, but showing too much leg in the workplace is a definite no-no.

Dresses made of stretchy or knit fabric that clings tightly to your body, calling attention to your breast and hips, should not be worn in the workplace. I repeat, should *not* be worn in the workplace! Pleated dresses or skirts normally fall better on a slim figure – remember that pleats can make your hips look larger.

...a dress 2 inches or more above the knee requires pantyhose.

Cleavage

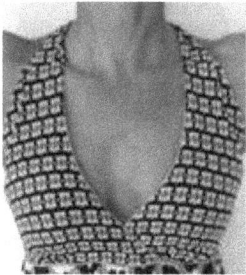

NEVER show cleavage at work. Not even a small portion of your breasts should be revealed – this applies to blouses, dresses and tops. Sagging breasts take away from one's silhouette, so make sure you have a properly fitted bra.

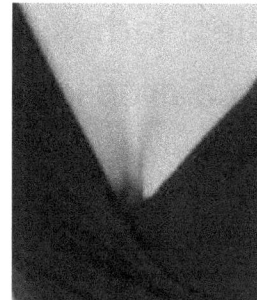

Your image in the office should reflect "professional," "serious about my career," "ready for a promotion."

Most of us believe that first lady Michelle Obama has made showing your arms a fashion statement. However, even if you have toned arms, be careful of wearing strappy dresses in the office. You may need a sweater or blazer to project a professional image depending on your workplace. The key is to limit showing too much skin.

> **Most of us believe that first lady Michelle Obama has made showing your arms a fashion statement.**

Pants

Ladies, ladies, ladies, please ensure your pants are ironed with a crease. Some pants have stitched creases that may require a quick press. Wrinkled, fresh-out-of-the dryer pants do not project a professional image. Save the comfy, fresh-out-of-the dryer pants for leisure wear outside the workplace.

Unless you are wearing capris or cropped pants, your ankles should not be showing. In other words, if the pants are too short or too tight (or *high waters* as the old-school crowd called them) let them go – donate them to your favorite charity. On the other hand, pants that are too long – hanging under your shoes, causing you to almost trip and fall – are not classy. Befriend a good tailor.

If your panty line is showing through your pants, wear a long jacket to cover your hips. Also, it is worth the investment to purchase underwear designed to show no panty lines. That is if you do not wear thong underwear.

If your panty line is showing through your pants, wear a long jacket to cover your hips.

Revealing any portion of your underwear, the crack of your butt or tattoos while sitting, bending or standing isn't classy. Caution is encouraged particularly when wearing hip-hugger pants or skirts. Solve the problem with a long jacket or a long T-shirt.

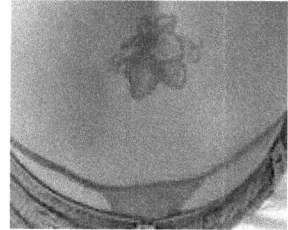

If you need to continuously pull your blouse down over your waistline, or pull your pants up on your hips, chances are the pants aren't appropriate for the workplace.

Tattoos

Another caution regarding displaying tattoos in the workplace: A CareerBuilder.com study found that 37 percent of human resources managers cite tattoos as the third physical attribute most likely to limit career potential. Non-ear piercings topped the list, followed by bad breath.

Executive career coach Meredith Haberfeld said that ink often can send the message to employers and clients that individuals are trying to rebel.

Leggings

Attention, ladies! Leggings are called "leggings" because they were created to warm or cover the legs. Leggings are not pants! Regardless of how sexy we believe we may look or whether we're a size 2 or size 22, leggings should *not* be worn as pants. *Unless, of course, you're exercising (see Lonnie Bush Fitness).*

Cover up leggings as you would cover up a pair of tights – both were created to cover the legs.

Regardless of how sexy we believe we look, leggings should not be worn as pants!

Jackets

We all know what having "junk in the trunk" means. Sometimes it can mean large hips, sometimes it can mean the stomach is protruding a little too far over the belt. Jackets with vents in the back combined with junk in the trunk can be problematic. If you look in the mirror and the vent behind you is standing at attention and you know it's supposed to be lying flat, the jacket is too small. The back vent rule also applies to skirts and dresses.

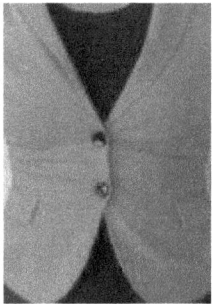 Another point regarding jackets: If you have fastened the buttons over your breasts or protruding stomach and the buttons look as if they are ready to pop off into 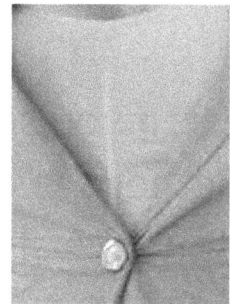 someone's eye, the jacket is too small. Take it off and give it away.

...if your button looks like it's ready to pop off into someone's eye, the jacket is too small.

Fabrics for the Seasons

Let's begin by noting that there is a difference between summer after-five and winter after-five fabric. Please refrain from wearing a summer fabric with a fur coat. If static cling is your friend for the evening, you have selected the wrong fabric. Boots and fur coats should be worn with winter fabrics such as beads, sequins, wool, knits, cashmere, thick silk and polyester. Yes, some polyester fabrics are classy. Thin silk or thin polyester fabrics are not appropriate in winter. I've observed women strolling in summer silk dresses wearing boots and fur coats. It was one of those "Um, um, um" moments.

Next, if you see lint balls forming on your fabric, evaluate whether the outfit needs to be dry cleaned or trashed. Oftentimes, lint balls form on inexpensive fabrics that were meant for minimal wear or clothing we've tried to wear too many times between dry cleaning.

If static cling is your friend for the evening, you have selected the wrong fabric.

Colors for Your Body Type

I have a cardinal rule for corporate America: Do not mix and match more than three colors. Although the fashion trends are encouraging a rainbow of colors with a variety of patterns, in corporate America you may be perceived as Bozo the Clown and risk not being recognized as a skilled professional. One would not wear a yellow and orange flowered blouse with a red pinstriped suit, however, the red pinstriped suit can be tasteful with a solid yellow or orange blouse. And always consider colors that enhance, versus clash with, your skin tone and hair color.

Finally ladies, remember that light-colored fabrics can add two to four dress sizes to your body. Anyone with a goal of looking slim should not wear coats, pants, skirts or dresses in white or cream. Floral, large polka dots and multicolor patterns also can make your body look larger than it is. Slimming colors are black, brown, navy, gray and burgundy. The majority of medium- to dark-colored solid fabrics are more slimming. Slimming patterns are vertical (up and down) versus horizontal (side to side) stripes.

Floral, large polka dots and multi-color patterns can make your body look larger than it is.

Hosiery

Fishnets or other patterned pantyhose are not professional for the workplace unless you are wearing them under a pantsuit. This is party hosiery and is suitable in a nightclub or party venue. Opaque or sheer stockings are more appropriate for the workplace.

Prevent snags, runs and lint balls with hand washing. Again, some items are not meant to last a lifetime. Finances may be tight, but go ahead and trash hosiery that has runs, lint balls and the like. Do not wear them! Reiterating a point made earlier in the section on dresses, bare legs are acceptable with a dress or skirt no more than 2 inches above the knees.

Trash hosiery that has runs, lint balls and the like.

Belts

When a woman is wearing a belt, her waist immediately attracts attention. Wider belts tend to attract more attention than narrow belts. Therefore, a woman with a larger waistline should be cautious of her belt selection. For the larger waistline, a narrow, non-stretchable belt creates a neater appearance. Stretch belts tend to create more of a bulge, or muffin top, around the waist creating a less attractive appearance.

Women with smaller waists can wear just about any kind of belt. However, I've often observed women with smaller waists wearing belts that dangle.

Dangling belts, as the one pictured above, take away from a neat appearance. When a small belt is too tight and you buy a medium, or a medium belt is too small and you buy a large, you end up with a belt that dangles in front of your outfit because it's too long. Sometimes a belt loop is not stitched too far on the side of the garment, allowing you to drape the dangling part of your belt into the loop. However, oftentimes an additional loop isn't available which prompted my invention – read on.

I generally experience the dangling-belt issue, so I invented a decorative crystal brooch, pictured to the left, that is used to secure the dangling or flapping end of a belt.

This belt brooch is available in three sizes and is available in various colors to coordinate with outfits. If you're interested in purchasing a belt brooch, please contact me at christaniocollection@yahoo.com.

In conclusion, I hope this book has enlightened your fashion sense and is helpful in your quest to be a professionally dressed fashionista. Take time daily to look in a full-length mirror before departing for work or any event. The mirror does provide a true reflection. Also, ask yourself, "Would I wear this outfit to meet with a company executive?" Be prepared for unannounced opportunities.

I encourage you to pass this information down to your daughters, granddaughters, nieces, mentees and other women in your life. Be further encouraged as you dress daily to remember that styles may change, but DRESSING CLASSY DOESN'T CHANGE!

May God bless you!

Your support is sincerely appreciated.

Contact me at christaniocollection@yahoo.com.

Remember to type in the subject line:

"DRESSING CLASSY DOESN'T CHANGE"

WORKS CITED:

Excerpts from: Federal Daily, News and Resource for Federal and Postal Employees, Dress code –Federal Soup: http://federalsoup.federaldaily.com/forum_posts.asp,*n.d.,#n.p*. 4 March 2013

Excerpts from: Marketplace Workplace Culture-Interview by Tess Vigeland, October 19, 2012: http://www.marketplace.org/topics/business/workplace-culture/tattoos-workplace-still-taboo.

Corporation name related to Corporate Dress Policy purposely not disclosed.